Kindness Countdown to Christmas

A Family Devotional

Angel Williams

ISBN: 979-8-9915886-0-7

DEDICATION

This book is dedicated in memory of my husband, Dennis Williams (1972-2023), and to all I love most - my family. For my son, Mason, I send this special message: You can accomplish anything you set your mind to. I hope you reach for the stars and grab them with both hands. Always remember, you *"can do all things through Christ who strengthens"* you (Philippians 4:13).

ACKNOWLEDGMENTS

Thank you to all my friends and family who believed in me, and who have encouraged me in my writing over the years. One incredibly special person who first encouraged my writing was my 5th grade teacher, Mrs. Eleanor Brown. As a former teacher myself, I hope teachers never underestimate the power they have in which to positively impact the life of a child forever.

Thank you, Christine Holder, for your inspiring illustration: you always bring a unique perspective.

Sandra Hendrix, thank you for allowing me to keep you busy helping me with the book cover – as if you weren't busy enough already. You are so amazingly talented.

Laurie, you are the best sister anyone could ever ask for. Despite everything you have going on, you still found time to help me edit my book. I can't begin to thank you enough for your encouragement and support.

Thank you, in advance, to everyone who purchases this book and helps to promote it. Together, we can make a positive difference in the world.

Introduction

As we enter the Christmas season, we often find ourselves immersed in the commercialism of Christmas, striving to find just the right present to put under the tree that will put a smile on our child's face. We may find ourselves overstimulated and stressed from the "hustle and bustle" of the season, which stores have the best sales, and all the busy calendar events we feel obligated to attend. We may even find ourselves striving to "keep up with the Joneses" by trying to find the popular, "sold out everywhere" hottest toys or latest up to date tech devices for our children, only to feel a sense of shame or guilt if we cannot or do not deliver. Somewhere amid it all, we lose sight of what truly matters, which is the "Christ" in "Christmas."

Generation after generation, parents have shared stories with children about Santa Claus, encouraging children to stay on Santa's "nice" list, and have even threatened children with lumps of coal in their stockings if they did not behave. The tradition of "Elf on a Shelf" has been gaining in popularity since 2005 with all the humorous antics the "elf" does as he or she moves about the house, "watching" children to see if they are staying on Santa's "nice" list.

Such practices, though seemingly harmless in nature, come with the subtle threat that children will not receive any presents for Christmas if they are not "good." From a parenting perspective, such threats are of no value to us if we are not prepared to act on them. Would a parent really deny their child a present for Christmas if their actions were less than perfect? For the purposes of this book, it is safe to assume that most parents would never withhold Christmas from their children. We understand that they are still young, learning, and that no one is perfect, - not even mom or dad!

The first gift of Christmas, Jesus Christ, was freely given. Therefore, should not the gifts we give, out of love and compassion during the Christmas season, also be freely given? Be this as it may, parents also have an obligation to raise decent, respectful, caring, and compassionate human beings - not children who feel a sense of entitlement or who take the gifts they receive for granted.

The premise of this book will be to help shift our focus from what we want for ourselves for Christmas, to the kindness we can do for others. In this book, you will find brief, daily family devotionals. Most devotionals will include portions of the biblical story of the birth of Christ, along with "kindness" challenges for you and your family to complete along the way as you work your way through the 25-day countdown to Christmas.

This book is intended to draw you closer together as a family, not add more stress to an already stressful time of year. Therefore, please give yourself grace if you, as a family, find there are some challenges you just are not able to complete this year. Even one act of kindness completed is better than none. Tomorrow is a brand-new day, and there is always next year for any challenges you find you were not able to complete this year.

You may also discover that you and/or your children have ideas for acts for kindness to complete that are not mentioned in this book. The challenges mentioned throughout the book are mere suggestions that closely align with the biblical passages mentioned.

It is also my hope that, outside of your close family unit, that your extended family, your church congregation, may work together to help complete some of these challenges as well. Working together, we can all make a positive difference in the lives of those around us, and we do not always have to spend money to do so. Even young children can make a difference in the lives of others, which is why this book is written in a family devotional-type format. I wish you and your family all the best as you work toward putting "Christ" back in "Christmas." I think you'll discover that, by creating a new family tradition of intentional kindness, the Christmas season will bring a richer, more rewarding experience for your family as well as the lives you touch.

May you and yours have a very Merry Christmas!

Note: Bible verses are from New International Version (2011).

December 1st

For today's devotional, we are going to take a minute to pause and reflect. In today's day and time, the likelihood of any of us ever seeing a heavenly angel descend from the sky to greet us is slim. However, God can place people in our lives to be "angels" in our time of need, and he can use us to be "angels" in the lives of others as well.

One of the first and best ways we can be an "angel" in the life of someone else is through the power of prayer.

James 5:16 states, *"Therefore confess your sins to each other and pray for each other so that you may be healed. The prayer of a righteous person is powerful and effective."*

Never underestimate the power of prayer.

Today's challenge is to, as a family, create a prayer list. Space has been provided in the back of this book for your prayer list. List anyone you may know who may be facing health issues, financial stress, grief and loss, marital issues, or concerns of which you may be aware. Please don't forget to add your church pastor and other community leaders to this list. They, too, need ongoing strength and encouragement.

Children: Do you know a child at your school who often sits or eats alone who could use your prayers? Is there someone at your school who could use some help in learning how to be kind to others? Is your teacher having a challenging year with students in your class who may not be listening to him or her? All these people could use your prayers.

Once you have created your list, commit to pray for everyone on your list, beginning today, as a family, every day between now and Christmas.

December 2nd

Mary was greatly troubled at his words and wondered what kind of greeting this might be. But the angel said to her, "Do not be afraid, Mary, you have found favor with God. You will conceive and give birth to a son, and you are to call him Jesus. He will be great and will be called the Son of the Most High. The Lord God will give him the throne of his father David, and he will reign over Jacob's descendants forever; his kingdom will never end."

"How will this be," Mary asked the angel, "since I am a virgin?"

Luke 1:29-34

From these verses, we know that Mary has been chosen to bring the Son of God into this world. To everyone else, however, within her society, she would have negatively been viewed as a pregnant, unwed mother. Can you imagine how frightening this must have been for Mary, and how worried she may have been that Joseph may not have accepted her as his wife once he learned she was pregnant?

Even today, there are young, unwed mothers who find themselves frightened and alone. They may feel they have no one to turn to and no one to ask for help. Even when they do ask for help on social media or other places, they often find themselves the subject of bullying and judgment.

With the state of our current economy, even in two parent households, with both parents working full-time, many families are struggling just to cover basic expenses and put food on the table. Can you imagine how much harder this may be for a young, single mother?

Daycare may take most of her income, and the cost of basic housing has really gone up. Every time her child is sick, and she must miss work to take care of them, this is even more money out of her pocket. This makes it challenging for her to provide healthy meal choices for her children, and numerous other things her children might need, such as money for school trips, birthday presents, and/or school supplies.

Our challenge for today is to think of ways you can help support a single mother. Parents, can you offer to watch her children for her so she can do her Christmas shopping or simply catch up on some sleep? Are there tasks she needs done around her home that she may not have the time, energy, tools, or experience to tackle? Can you help sponsor her family for Christmas or take her a special care package? Single parents may not receive anything for Christmas unless their children are old enough to make or buy them something.

Children: Is there a child in your class who never has money for extra school purchases, such as for book fairs, field trips, or even a hot school lunch? If you, yourself, live in a single parent household, is there something special you can do for your parent to help him or her out around the house? Can you make something special for your mom, dad, or guardian to put under the tree so they know how much you love and treasure them? Do you have clothes you have outgrown or toys you no longer play with that could help another child? Even a drawing or a loving note could make an amazing gift for your parent.

There are a multitude of ways to help support a single parent. Please take a few minutes, as a family, to brainstorm what you can do to complete this challenge.

Reminder: Pray over your prayer list you created on Day 1.

Note: Brainstorming pages for each day have been provided at the end of this book.

December 3rd

> *The angel answered, "The Holy Spirit will come on you, and the power of the Most High will overshadow you. So the holy one to be born will be called the 'Son of God.' Even Elizabeth your relative is going to have a child in her old age, and she who was said to be unable to conceive is in her sixth month. For no word from God will ever fail."*
>
> *"I am the Lord's servant," Mary answered. "May your word to me be fulfilled." Then the angel left her.*
>
> Luke 1:35-38

In these verses, we can see that the angel mentions a relative of Mary, named Elizabeth, who has also been blessed with a pregnancy in her "old age." For the backstory here, Elizabeth and her husband Zechariah, who was a priest, had longed for children of their own for an exceedingly long time. When they had nearly given up hope, God blessed them with a son, who would later be known as "John the Baptist." John would later fulfill a mighty purpose by baptizing Jesus, the Son of God, and introducing baptism to others as well.

When we think about Elizabeth and Zechariah, we can picture all the years of grief they must have endured by watching all their other family members and friends have children, while painfully wondering why the same couldn't happen for them. I am sure they were overjoyed when they finally found out they were going to have a child, but I am sure that the wait they went through was quite challenging.

During the Christmas Season, we tend to feel grief and loss even more strongly. All of those who have ever longed for children, but have not been able to have them, may feel a powerful sense of loss during Christmas. They do not have the child they have always dreamed of shopping for or surprising with gifts under the tree. They see all the social media posts from friends with photos of children in cute Christmas outfits, such as "baby's first Christmas," and wonder why that cannot be them.

Others may have had babies who were "born sleeping," or they may have faced other significant losses, such as a child, spouse, parent, or other close loved one who may have passed away from a serious illness or tragic accident.

Children in foster care may be facing their first Christmas away from their biological parents, grandparents, and even their siblings, which also creates significant grief and loss.

When you have gone through such loss, the first holidays without your loved ones can be the most challenging.

With this in mind, our challenge for today is to acknowledge someone who may be struggling with some form of grief and loss this year. Is there someone who comes to mind who may benefit from a phone call, a card, or a special care package to let them know they are not alone, and that you are thinking of them?

Children: Is there someone at your school who may have lost a parent, a sibling, or who may be in foster care? Is there something special you can do for them to let them know you care?

As a family, please brainstorm who you would like to connect with that may be struggling with grief and loss. If you, yourself, have faced grief and loss this year, is there something kind you can do for yourselves, such as make and eat your favorite treat, or watch your favorite movie?

Reminder: Pray over the prayer list you created. You may discover a need to add someone new to your prayer list who is struggling with grief and loss.

December 4th

> *This is how the birth of Jesus the Messiah came about: His mother Mary was pledged to be married to Joseph, but before they came together, she was found to be pregnant through the Holy Spirit. Because Joseph her husband was faithful to the law, and yet did not want to expose her to public disgrace, he had in mind to divorce her quietly.*
>
> *But after he had considered this, an angel of the Lord appeared to him in a dream and said, "Joseph son of David, do not be afraid to take Mary home as your wife, because what is conceived in her is from the Holy Spirit. She will give birth to a son, and you are to give him the name Jesus, because he will save his people from their sins."*
>
> Matthew 1:18-21

When we read these passages above, we can picture how confused Joseph must have been when he learned the woman he was planning to marry had become pregnant. It was likely also challenging for him to believe the words of the angel who visited him, and to accept that Mary had become pregnant by the Holy Spirit. He trusted these words and chose to still take Mary to be his wife.

Had Joseph not agreed to take Mary as his wife, in the period these events occurred, Mary could have been shunned by her community, which basically means that no one would have helped her with basic survival needs of food, shelter, clothing, or friendship. She also could have been severely injured by others or worse. If Joseph had not stepped up, the life of Mary's unborn child, Jesus, could have been at grave risk.

Joseph then becomes the "hero" here by accepting the role of "stepfather" and becoming the "father" he did not have to be.

With this in mind, our challenge for today is to do something kind for a loving father, stepfather, "father" mentor, adoptive father, foster father. If there is someone in your life you know who chose to be a wonderful loving "father" to a child, even when they did not have to, please let them know today how very much appreciated they are. Like single mothers we spoke about, there are also single fathers out there who could use some love and support.

Children: Is there something special you can do your father or a special "father" figure in your life? A nice drawing or note can be just as nice for fathers as they are for mothers.

What can you, as a family, do to support a father in need?

Reminder: Pray over your prayer list today.

December 5th

> *All this took place to fulfill what the Lord had said through the prophet: "The virgin will conceive and give birth to a son, and they will call him Immanuel (which means "God with us").*
>
> *When Joseph woke up, he did what the angel of the Lord had commanded him and took Mary home as his wife.*
>
> Matthew 1: 22-24

As we mentioned, while exploring the passages for our last challenge, Joseph chose to proceed with his plan of marriage to Mary. Becoming married, to someone you genuinely care about and respect, and who cares about and respects you as well, can be an incredibly beautiful thing. It can also be frightening, full of uncertainties, and come with financial challenges and hardships, particularly for young couples just starting out in the early years of their marriage.

The Christmas season can be very magical, and it is one where a lot of weddings tend to occur.

Our challenge for today is to do something kind for someone you know who may be getting married this season. Is there a young couple who could use some encouragement and support as they begin their new journey together? Is there a couple who is struggling in their marriage right now who could use a friend?

What can you, as a family, do to help support a married couple, or soon to be married couple, in need?

Parents, is there anything you can do to strengthen your own marriage if you are married?

Children: If your parents or grandparents are married, is there something special you can do for them, such as make them a loving card, surprise them with a special dinner or treat you are able to safely prepare, or giving them some space and time alone?

Reminder: Pray over your prayer list from Day 1. You may even find your list is growing longer as we continue our kindness countdown to Christmas.

December 6th

> *Love is patient, love is kind. It does not envy, it does not boast, it is not proud. It does not dishonor others, it is not self-seeking, it is not easily angered, it keeps no record of wrongs. Love does not delight in evil but rejoices with the truth. It always protects, always trusts, always hopes, always perseveres.*
>
> 1 Corinthians 13:4-7

While we near the day where we traditionally celebrate Jesus's birth, we will take a break from our biblical Christmas story, and explore, more in-depth, what the Bible has to say about kindness.

What is mentioned in the verses above is not always easy to achieve, as none of us are perfect, but it is something to aim for. As we move through our kindness challenges in this book, we should do so, not in a way that is "boastful," cause "envy," or that would "dishonor" someone, but do so simply out of the kindness of our hearts.

This passage in 1 Corinthians goes on to say, in verse 13: *"And now these three remain: faith, hope, and love. But the greatest of these is love."*

As we reflect on these verses today, what act of kindness can we do today that will demonstrate our ability to be "patient"? Can we be kind to others while driving in traffic? Can we be more patient with our children as they try to complete a task (e.g., putting on their shoes, getting dressed, etc.)?

Children: Can you show more patience for our parents as they prepare meals for you, and while you wait for them to finish something before giving you their undivided attention?

Is there something you can do today, either on your own or as a family, that can let someone know they are loved, even if it is with a simple note or phone call?

With how busy and stressed people can become during the Christmas season, extra patience and kindness can go a long way to brightening someone's day.

Reminder: Pray over your prayer list today.

December 7th

> *Be kind and compassionate to one another, forgiving each other, just as in Christ God forgave you.*
>
> Ephesians 4:32
>
> .

One of the biggest acts of kindness we can do is to exercise the power of forgiveness. The ability to forgive can be incredibly challenging, particularly if someone did something to us that hurt us very badly. Sometimes, we also struggle to forgive ourselves if we have done something we are not proud of or that may have hurt someone else.

To forgive does not necessarily mean that we forget a wrongdoing, or even mean that we need to allow toxic, abusive people to play active roles in our lives.

Forgiveness is a way of letting go of our anger, resentment, grudge, or even sadness that may revolve around hurtful things others have done to us. If we can find compassion for those who have wronged us, by understanding what pain from their past may have caused them to act the way they did, then, with this understanding, forgiveness becomes possible.

Even more challenging than forgiving someone else, however, is the ability to show ourselves the same kindness of forgiveness. All of us have made mistakes, and we have all done something, at some point, that may have been hurtful to someone else. We may have even asked people we offended to forgive us, or told them how sorry we were, but may still hold it against ourselves.

Our challenge for today is to forgive others and to forgive ourselves. Is there something you need to get off your chest and talk to someone about? Do you need to tell someone you are sorry for hurting their feelings, or for something else you may have done? Parents, is there a parenting mistake you made along the way for which you struggle to forgive yourself?

Children: Is there a lie you may have told, or something else you may have been hiding for which you would like your parents or someone else to forgive you? Is there someone who may have hurt you that you need to find in your heart to forgive? If so, please talk to your parents about this situation so that they can help you through this. If you are uncomfortable talking about this with your parents, please talk with another trusted adult, such as your teacher or school counselor.

Forgiveness can take time, and it may not happen today. For significant pain that others may have caused us, or that you may have caused someone else, it can take a lifetime to fully work through. Forgiveness is, however, one of the greatest acts of kindness we can give to ourselves and to others.

As mentioned above, forgiving someone does not mean you need to allow toxic, abusive people back into your life. It does not even mean you need to have a conversation with them, unless you are the one who wronged them and need to acknowledge your wrongdoing to them. Forgiveness is a way of letting go of our past, of our pain, and our hurt, so we can find peace within ourselves.

The Bible commands us, in Mark 12:30, to "...*love your neighbor as yourself.*" If we are to love our neighbors as ourselves, this would imply that we are to love ourselves as well. Using this logic, shouldn't we show ourselves the same grace, compassion, and love regarding the ability to forgive ourselves, just as we are expected to forgive others?

What steps can you take today to work toward forgiveness? Have you asked others to forgive you? Have you asked God to forgive you? Have you asked God to help you forgive someone else?

This kindness challenge may be one of the most difficult to accomplish, but you may find it to be one that is necessary and needed the most. Best wishes as you work through this challenge.

Forgiving someone who has wronged you may well be the best Christmas gift either of you will ever receive!

Reminder: Please remember to pray over your prayer list today as well.

December 8th

Dear children, let us not love with words or speech but with actions and in truth.

1 John 3:18

Whoever is kind to the poor lends to the Lord, and he will reward them for what they have done.

Proverbs 19:17

Have you ever heard the saying, "The kindness you put out into the world has a way of coming back to you?" This is, essentially, what Proverbs 19:17 is saying here. However, should we show kindness simply because there may be a reward from doing so, or because it is the right thing to do? For instance, if we find someone's wallet on the ground, do we return it because we hope they will give us money, or because it is the right and just thing to do? If we were the ones who lost our wallet, wouldn't we want someone to return it to us?

In Luke 6:31, we are told, *"Do to others as you would have them do to you."* This is the "Golden Rule" that is also mentioned in Matthew 7:12. This "Golden Rule" can serve as our guiding light throughout life and our beacon to why it is so important to always be kind.

Kindness is not just something we say with our words, but with our actions and deeds. For instance, we can say that it is wrong to bully, but do we back this up with our actions by not bullying others or helping others to stand up against bullies? Do we tell someone that we love them but then turn around and do something unkind to them?

What act of kindness can you do today that would demonstrate how you are a follower of the "Golden Rule?" Can you hold a door open for someone? Can you let someone go in front of you in line who may have trouble standing, or who may have fewer items? Can you let someone in front of you in traffic, just as you would like someone to do for you?

Children: Can you invite someone to play with you at recess, or sit with you at your lunch table who may not have a friend, just as you would like someone to do for you when you need a friend?

Is there something you can do, as a family, to treat another family the way you would like to be treated? What other ideas can you think of to spread kindness?

Christmas can be a very magical time of year to help spread kindness and cheer. There will likely be several opportunities to demonstrate your following of the

"Golden Rule" this holiday season. It is also a wonderful time of year to help those who are less fortunate than us.

Reminder: Please remember to also pray over your prayer list today.

December 9th

> **In those days Caesar Augustus issued a decree that a census should be taken of the entire Roman world. And everyone went to their own town to register.**
>
> Luke 2:23

Now that we are growing closer to Christmas Day, we will return to our biblical Christmas story.

This passage above, in reference to the census, is a head count for how many people live in each household. This was ordered under the presumption that the information would be used to collect taxes from everyone.

Now, most of us know about how taxes are withheld from our paychecks, how we pay property taxes for our vehicles and homes, and how we need to file taxes every year with the government, but what "tax" does the Bible say we are to pay to God and/or our church?

In Leviticus 27:30, we are told, *"a tithe from everything from the land, whether grain from the soil, or fruit from the trees, belongs to the Lord; it is holy to the Lord."*

In some biblical verses, and, in other Bible prints, this "tithe," as can be seen in the story of Cain and Able, is our first and best produce to the Lord. In Deuteronomy, a "tithe" is described as a "tenth," which is why many churches will talk about giving 10% of your gross earnings to the church. After all, this money is needed to help pay for the building, building repairs, salaries for your minister and staff, utilities, supplies, and any community outreach services or programs your church provides.

While this is all fine and good, and necessary regarding keeping a church in operation, the Bible also states in 2 Corinthians 9:7 that, *"Each of you should give what you have decided in your heart to give, not reluctantly or under compulsion, for God loves a cheerful giver."*

For those living paycheck to paycheck, barely able to afford rent and put food on the table, it can, of course, be challenging to be a "cheerful giver." When tithes were first discussed in the Bible, it was referencing food that was grown, or "lambs" that were raised. Therefore, if or when you find you are unable to give monetarily to your church, are there other things you can do to help support your church and community?

Can you "cheerfully" give of your time? Can you help teach a class? Can you donate food from your garden to those who need it?

Children: Can you collect pennies to give to the church, or donate drawing paper and materials for Sunday School classes?

During winter months and the Christmas season, there is an abundance of community needs your church will not be able to meet alone without your help and support.

As a family, try to brainstorm ways you can help "tithe" to your church. If you are not presently in a church, then perhaps sit down as a family and make a list of what you would like to find in a church. Research the churches in your area that you think will most meet the list your family has created. Many churches host exciting events this time of year that may create opportunities for you to visit some churches until you find the one that feels right for you and your family.

Reminder: Please also remember to pray over your prayer list today.

December 10th

So Joseph also went up from the town of
Nazareth in Galilee to Judea, to Bethlehem
the town of David, because he belonged to
the house and line of David. He went there to
register with Mary, who was pledged to be
married to him and was expecting a child.

Luke 2:4-5

After Mary and Joseph learned that they would be
traveling from Nazareth to Bethlehem, they would have
had to gather the provisions they would need for their
long journey ahead. Biblical scholars estimate that their
journey would have taken them anywhere between 4-7
days. On the way, they would have crossed over hills,
valleys, mountains, a desert, and rough and dusty terrain,
all while Mary was pregnant.

Over the next few days, the focus of our challenges will revolve around the challenges Mary and Joseph likely would have faced on their journey.

For today's challenge, we will focus on transportation. It is presumed that Mary and Joseph used a donkey to help them on their journey, as that is what was commonly used during that period. We do not know if Joseph already had the donkey, or if he had to somehow acquire one. If they did not at least have a donkey to help them carry their supplies, or a cart of some sort, then we can imagine how much more challenging this journey may have been.

Fast forward to current times; many people struggle with transportation needs, particularly in areas where there is not easy access to public transportation. Many people struggle with finding transportation to go pick up their medicine from the pharmacy, go to doctor appointments, or to access food from a food bank. Some may also not be able to have visits with their children in foster care due to not having transportation, while others may need to put their car in the shop for repairs, but not have a ride back home or to work.

For today's challenge, is there anything you can do, as a family, to help someone meet a transportation need. If it is not someone you know well enough to feel safe offering a ride, can you go pick something up for them that they need? Can you help them find resources in their area that could help them meet their transportation needs?

Children: Is there a child who rides your school bus who may seem scared or needs a friend to sit with? Is there a child in your extracurricular activities, or who would like to join such activities, but cannot make it because they do not have transportation?

As a family, please brainstorm ways you can help meet a transportation need for someone you know.

Reminder: Pray over your prayer list today.

December 11th

> *Then the King will say to those on his right, "Come, you who are blessed by my Father; take your inheritance, the kingdom prepared for you since the creation of the world. For I was hungry and you gave me something to eat, I was thirsty and you gave me something to drink, I was a stranger and you invited me in, I needed clothes and you clothed me, I was sick and you looked after me, I was in prison and you came to visit me."*
>
> Matthew 25:34-36

While Mary and Joseph were preparing for their journey to Bethlehem, we can assume that they needed to pack food to sustain them throughout their journey. We can also reasonably assume that there were other families making this journey as well. It is possible that individuals shared campfires and food to make sure no one went hungry, and that all safely survived the journey. In multiple places throughout the Bible, God commands us to feed the hungry.

So, for the purpose of today's challenge, we will focus on feeding the hungry. According to *nokidhungry.org*, based on 2022 USDA statistics, "as many as 13 million children (about twice the population of Arizona) in the United States live in 'food insecure' homes."

Given the current state of the economy in the United States, along with global economic issues and food shortages, it would be fair to assume that these numbers may be even higher. In the United States, there are many families and individuals who make just enough above the poverty line to not qualify for government assistance or free/reduced school lunches, but not enough to comfortably afford housing, utilities, childcare, transportation, or even food for their families.

According to Education Data Initiative's report, "*School Lunch Debt Statistics*," last updated in January of 2024, "The national public school meal debt is $262 million a year." There are an estimated, "30.4 million students (about the population of Texas)" who "can't afford their school meals."

In other words, unless you are blessed to live in a school district that provides every student with free breakfast and lunch meals, there are children right in your very school who cannot afford to eat. There may even be someone on your very street struggling to feed their family.

The world hunger issue is too large for one person, or one family, to solve, but everyone can do something. One place to start is to learn not to take the food we have for granted, and to be appreciative of the food we are offered, as there are many who will go without food tonight. Millions of children, all over the world, will go to bed hungry tonight.

As a family, what can you do to help meet someone's hunger needs? Is there one person you can help? Can you help provide a Christmas meal to a family in need?

Children: Is there a child in your school you can help who may not have money for lunch or snacks? Are there special school food days where money is needed for things like a snow cone or pretzel, and you see someone going without? There are some amazing child "heroes" who took creative approaches for helping to pay for student lunch balances at their school. Never underestimate what one child has the ability to accomplish.

Helping one person, or even one family, may not seem like much in the grand scheme of things, but to that one person or family, it can make all the difference.

Reminder: Pray over your prayer list today.

December 12th

> Then the King will say to those on his right, "Come, you who are blessed by my Father; take your inheritance, the kingdom prepared for you since the creation of the world. For I was hungry and you gave me something to eat, I was thirsty and you gave me something to drink, I was a stranger and you invited me in, I needed clothes and you clothed me, I was sick and you looked after me, I was in prison and you came to visit me."
>
> Matthew 25:34-36

For today's challenge, we will use the same passages as we did yesterday, but our focus for today will be on providing a drink for the thirsty.

Since part of Mary and Joseph's journey involved crossing through a desert, it would be reasonable to assume that they also packed a supply of water to take with them on their journey.

Many of us are familiar with struggles in developing countries regarding access to clean drinking water. However, did you know that, according to a March 2023 report from the U.S. Water Alliance and DigDeep, over two million Americans do not have access to basic access to safe drinking water and sanitation. Even today, many Americans do not have running water inside their homes. According to this same report, an "additional 44 million may have indoor plumbing, but their water systems have been in violation of the Safe Water Drinking Act." These statistics may not even include homeless individuals who would not have easy access to clean drinking water.

In Missouri, there is a Get the Lead Out of School Drinking Water Act. Many school districts have replaced water fountains with water bottle filling stations to help filter the water. However, there are still students who come to school without water bottles to refill, and numerous medical reports reference how severely children can, and do, become dehydrated during a school day.

For today's challenge, what can you do to provide clean drinking water to someone in need?

Children: Can you donate a new water bottle to a child in your class who may not have one? Can you, as a family, donate water to a homeless shelter? Do you ever offer a cold bottle of water to your delivery drivers or sanitation workers on a sweltering day?

As a family, please brainstorm ways you can help provide a drink for the thirsty. I am sure anyone struggling to meet such a basic need would be very grateful for your help, especially during the Christmas season.

Reminder: Pray over your prayer list.

December 13th

> *Then the King will say to those on his right, "Come, you who are blessed by my Father; take your inheritance, the kingdom prepared for you since the creation of the world. For I was hungry and you gave me something to eat, I was thirsty and you gave me something to drink, I was a stranger and you invited me in, I needed clothes and you clothed me, I was sick and you looked after me, I was in prison and you came to visit me."*
>
> Matthew 25:34-36

For today's challenge, we are now going to look more closely at verse 36 of the passage above and explore ways in which we can provide clothing for those in need.

Now, in biblical times, people likely did not have closets and dressers full of clothes like many people have today. It would not have been practical for them to do so, nor would they have had room to store that many belongings, particularly not for Mary and Joseph while on their journey to Bethlehem.

If Mary and Joseph were fortunate enough to afford a second outfit, they may have carried a change of clothes with them. However, clothes were expensive in those times, and many people may have only had one outfit to wear, especially while traveling.

While on such rough journeys, however, we can imagine how easily a tunic or robe could become torn, stained, or worn out. This would create a need for more clothing that may not have been easily available, which may be one reason providing clothing for others is mentioned in the Bible. Handing over an extra garment to someone in need would have been a great show of kindness considering how challenging it was to afford such garments during this period.

In our world today, there continues to be a need to provide clothing for others. Every day, a child enters the foster care system, very often with only the clothes on their backs. There are homeless individuals who would like to apply for work, but they may lack suitable clothing to be taken seriously when trying to apply for a job. There are women and children who have escaped domestic violence, having left all their belongings behind while attempting to start a new life. There are even people in hospitals and nursing homes with no clothes to change into, except for hospital gowns or scrubs.

What can you and your family do to help provide clothing for someone in need? Do you have any clean, gently used clothing you can donate? Are there any new clothes you bought, but never wore, that could bless someone else?

Could you help sponsor new clothes, underwear, pajamas, or socks for a child in foster care?

Children: Do you have clothing you no longer wear that you are able to donate? I am sure a nice toy or stuffed animal you no longer play with could help put a smile on another child's face as well this Christmas season.

As a family, please discuss ways you can help meet this need.

Reminder: Pray over your prayer list today.

December 14th

> *When he had finished washing their feet, he put on his clothes and returned to his place. "Do you understand what I have done for you?" he asked them. "You call me 'Teacher' and 'Lord,' and rightly so, for that is what I am. Now that I, your Lord and Teacher, have washed your feet, you also should wash one another's feet. I have set you an example that you should do as I have done for you."*
>
> John 13:12-15

In biblical times, the shoes most worn, if a person wore shoes, were sandals. It would be easy to imagine how sore and dirty the feet of Mary and Joseph would have been after such a long journey to Bethlehem.

The scripture passage above is referencing a time when Jesus washed the feet of his disciples. His disciples were uncertain how to respond to Jesus doing this, as such an action was one usually taken by a servant, not someone they believed to be their Lord. This passage, as Jesus demonstrated here, is another fine example of the Golden Rule: treating others the way you would like to be treated.

It also demonstrates how everyone should be treated equally, with no person higher or lower than another.

For today's challenge, however, we will focus on providing shoes to someone in need. As mentioned in the last challenge, every day children come into foster care without any shoes. One out of every three children living in the United States lives in poverty and may not be able to afford shoes that properly fit them. So many children are unable to participate in sports because they cannot afford the necessary shoes to do so.

According to *globalgiving.org*, and a variety of other sources, nearly 300 million children in the world are without shoes. There are many homeless individuals also in need of shoes, as well as elderly in nursing homes who could benefit from a pair of warm, slip-proof slippers.

There are numerous medical and physical challenges that can result from individuals not having proper shoes to wear. For children who must go barefoot, due to lack of shoes, this can cause them to become susceptible to injuries, parasites, or other infections. For those with diabetes, not having proper shoes can create issues with neuropathy pain and diabetic ulcers. Having proper footwear can go a long way toward preventing chronic pain.

As a family, can you brainstorm ways you can help provide shoes for someone in need? Can you help sponsor a new pair of shoes for a foster child? Do you have any gently used shoes you can donate?

Children: Do you have an outgrown pair of soccer cleats, baseball cleats, or ballet slippers that could help another child participate in a sport they may not have been able to do otherwise?

As a family, can you help your church or school organize a shoe drive?

It is amazing how something we may take for granted, an outgrown pair of shoes, could be the blessing someone is hopeful to receive this Christmas season.

Reminder: Pray over your prayer list today.

December 15th

> **What good is it, my brothers and sisters, if someone claims to have faith but has no deeds? Can such faith save them? Suppose a brother or a sister is without clothes and daily food. If one of you says to them, "Go in peace; keep warm and well fed," but does nothing about their physical needs, what good is it? In the same way, faith by itself, if it is not accompanied by action, is dead.**
>
> James 2:14-17

Throughout our daily challenges, thus far, we have been encouraged to create and pray over our prayer list. As mentioned on the first day of our countdown to Christmas journey, prayer can sometimes be the greatest gift of kindness we can do for someone. There are times where certain situations are out of our own power and control to change. However, there are also other needs we may be aware of that we do have the ability to help change.

This passage above demonstrates how there are times where our faith or prayer alone is not enough, if not also paired with our actions or deeds that would help meet that need.

For today's challenge, we will focus on helping to provide warmth for someone in need. As Mary and Joseph traveled to Bethlehem, they likely encountered chilly temperatures, particularly at night, as well as rain. They would have needed warm, wool clothing and blankets to survive such elements.

Now let us look at how the need for warmth impacts us today. Based on a 2023 report from the Department of Housing and Urban Development, there were over 653,000 homeless individuals in the United States. For those living in colder climates, it would be easy to imagine how challenging it would be for them to stay warm during the winter, particularly without the aid of warm clothing, coats, and blankets. This is not even considering those who have housing, but cannot afford heat, or those who live in housing that does not provide sufficient heat. It also does not account for current power grid struggles many parts of the United States are facing, or the likelihood of power outages due to storms and other causes that could impact someone's ability to stay warm.

As a family, can you brainstorm ways you can help provide warmth for someone this Christmas season? Do you have sleeping bags you no longer need that could be donated to a homeless person?

Can you donate warm sweaters, scarves, hats, or gloves? Do you have a warm blanket you can help donate, or warm coats you no longer wear? Can your church or school help organize a coat, hat, or glove drive?

Children: Is there a child in your school you have noticed who does not have a coat on a frigid day? If so, is there a coat of yours that you have outgrown that may be just what they need to stay warm during this winter and holiday season?

As mentioned with our food challenge, no one person or family can meet such a large need for everyone, but everyone can do something to help someone. It may not seem like much in the grand scheme of things, but, for that one person you are helping, it will mean the world to them.

Reminder: Pray over your prayer list today.

December 16th

If our assumption is correct, in that other people, besides Mary and Joseph, also made the journey to Bethlehem for the required census, then we can also reasonably assume that widows and orphans made this journey as well. Can you picture how hard such a journey would have been for someone who had no one to help them along the way, or to even help them find where they were going? We can only hope that others on this journey would have stepped in to assist widows and orphans, just as God has commanded us to do.

For today's challenge, we will explore ways we can help meet the needs of widows and orphans. For this challenge, we will include widowers as well. Foster children are also often categorized as orphans who need our help and support.

According to an April 2023 Census Bureau report, in the United States, there are an estimated 3.2 million orphaned children, and there are nearly 450,000 orphans in the foster care system. Of that number, over 100,000 children (about the seating capacity of the Los Angeles Memorial Coliseum) are awaiting adoptive homes.

There are also nearly 12 million widows and widowers in the United States.

As stated previously in this book, Christmas time can be incredibly challenging for those who are mourning the loss of a spouse, their parent(s), or who have been removed from everything they know while being placed in the foster care system. There are elderly people sitting in their homes or nursing homes, all alone, with no one to visit them. There are orphans/foster children who feel abandoned, thinking no one cares. Some may even find themselves sleeping in a Children's Services office or a shelter because safe placement homes are particularly challenging to find this time of year.

As a family, can you brainstorm ways you can help support an orphan or a widow/widower this holiday season? Can you visit a nursing home to offer company to someone who otherwise would not have a visitor?

Could you and your family, or your church, go sing Christmas Carols for them?

Is there a widow or widower you know who you can visit in their home? Your visit, and any special presents or treats you bring them, might be the only gift they will receive this year.

Can you help sponsor an orphan/foster child for Christmas this year? There are many who donate toys for younger children, but appropriate gifts for older youth are often an unmet need. Could you donate a gift card to a place a teen might like to go, or even a board or card game older youth might enjoy playing?

Children: Can you think of something you can give or do that could help a widow or orphan have a reason to smile this Christmas?

Reminder: Pray over your prayer list today.

December 17ᵗʰ

Do not forget to show hospitality to strangers, for by so doing some people have shown hospitality to angels without knowing it.

Hebrews 13:2

For those who are led by the Spirit of God are the children of God.

Romans 8:14

While Mary and Joseph were on their journey to Bethlehem, it is probable that they met and interacted with strangers along the way.

In our everyday lives, when we go to church, our school, enter a grocery store, or go for a walk, we often cross paths with people we have never met, or people we do not know well.

While granted, in the world we live in today, we need to exercise a certain amount of caution when interacting with strangers, there is also a need or expectation to be kind.

For instance, if you see someone, with their hands full, is about to go through a door, the kind thing to do would be to hold the door open for them. If you see an elderly or handicapped person empty their cart of items into their car, the kind thing to do would be to offer to take their cart for them. If you see someone crying, the kind thing to do would be to ask them if they are okay.

Sometimes, if we listen closely to the Holy Spirit, that still, small voice inside of us, He will lead us to the right place, at the right time, to help someone in need, whether with our actions, our kind words, or our prayers.

For our challenge today, as a family, talk about any acts of kindness you may have done today for a stranger, not because you had to, or because of any challenges in this book, but because you felt led to do so. How did completing that act of kindness make you feel? How do you think it made the person you helped feel?

Is there an act of kindness you felt led to do, but for whatever reason, you did not act on? Was there a moment today where you did not exercise kindness toward a stranger or anyone else? What do you think you could have done differently? This family conversation is for reflection purposes only, and to further explore ways we can be kind to others in our everyday lives and interactions. This is intended to be a safe, open discussion, for everyone and is not intended to create shame for any actions we wish we could have done differently. We are human, and everyone makes mistakes. However, reflection is an important part of improvement and growth toward becoming the best versions of ourselves we are meant to be.

Children: What did you do to show someone kindness today? What would you like to do tomorrow to show someone kindness that you may not have been able to do today?

George Matthew Adams, a famous American newspaper columnist from the late 1800's and early 1900's, had this to say about kindness and Christmas: "Let us remember that the Christmas heart is a giving heart, a wide-open heart that thinks of others first."

Reminder: Pray over your prayer list.

December 18th

Offer hospitality to one another without grumbling. Each of you should use whatever gift you have received to serve others, as faithful stewards of God's grace in its various forms.

.

1 Peter 4:9-10

Mary and Joseph completed their journey to Bethlehem. It is reasonable to assume, after their long journey, that they arrived very tired, hungry, and dirty. It is easy to imagine that the first thing on their mind was to find a nice, warm place to rest. The Bible does not tell us how long Mary and Joseph were in Bethlehem before it was time for Mary to give birth to Jesus. What it does tell us, in Luke 2:6, is that the time for Jesus to be born happened while they were there. In Luke 2:7, it mentions that there was no room for them in the "inn."

When we picture an "inn," by present day standards, we tend to imagine some sort of hotel. Doesn't most every Christmas play and movie we have seen, regarding the traditional, biblical Christmas story, depict an angry innkeeper turning Mary and Joseph away as they frantically search for a room?

Interestingly, the Hebrew interpretation of the word "inn" is "night resting place," and the Greek interpretation of the word "inn" is "guest room" or "lodging." Some biblical scholars believe that Mary and Joseph attempted to stay with one of Joseph's relatives, which was customary during that period, particularly for a pregnant relative. However, since there were no guest rooms available in their relative's home, it is believed that Mary and Joseph may have had to stay on the lower level of the house, which was also customary for animals to be housed.

Whichever the case may be, we can interpret Luke 2:7 to mean that Mary and Joseph struggled to find a comfortable place to stay while Mary was preparing to give birth to baby Jesus. We can also infer that the only place that was available to them is where animals were also kept.

In consideration of Mary and Joseph's struggles to find suitable shelter in their time of need, along with the passage above regarding providing "hospitality," our challenge for today will revolve around providing shelter or "hospitality" for someone in need.

As a family, can you brainstorm ways you may be able to help provide shelter for someone in need? Do you have a family member or friend who may be spending their Christmas holiday all alone that might enjoy spending time with your family?

Is there a lonely neighbor who might like to join your family for a holiday meal?

Is there a foreign exchange student or foster youth who has aged out of the system, whose college dorms may be closed for the holiday break and may be faced with having nowhere to go?

Is there a foster family who may need respite for their foster children because the court system will not allow them to take the children with them out of state as they go to visit their loved ones for the holidays?

Anytime we invite individuals we don't know into our home, does, of course, necessitate a need for caution. Therefore, if this is not something you feel led to do, or are not comfortable doing, are there other ways you can help? Could you help sponsor a hotel room for a night for someone who needs shelter or donate to your church so they can help someone who needs it?

Children: If you and your family are offering hospitality to someone in your home, what can you do to help? Can you help clean your room and your house, let someone borrow your bed, if needed, or help your family prepare the food that will be needed?

When everyone works together, such work can be accomplished much more quickly. The rest of the time can be spent simply enjoying the Christmas season as a family.

Reminder: Pray over your prayer list today.

December 19th

The righteous care for the needs of their animals, but the kindest acts of the wicked are cruel.

Proverbs 12:10

.

As mentioned in our last challenge, the place Mary and Joseph were given to stay, as she prepared to give birth to Jesus, was in a place that also housed animals.

For today's challenge, we will explore what the Bible says regarding caring for animals and ways we may be able to show kindness to animals.

In Proverbs 12:10, we can see that we are commanded to care for animals kindly and that only the "wicked" treat their animals cruelly. In fact, caring for animals is mentioned in a variety of verses throughout the Bible.

Deuteronomy 5:14, which is a passage about how, "*the seventh day is a sabbath to the Lord your God*," and it supposed to be a day of rest. Even animals are included in this passage, with a command for them to not do any work on this day as well.

Leviticus 25:6-7 discusses providing food for your animals, along with your family and members of your household, from the crops of your land.

Our challenge for today will, therefore, be to explore ways we can help care for an animal.

As a family, please brainstorm ways you can help care for a needy animal.

Could you foster an animal from a shelter so they do not have to spend the holiday inside a lonely, cold kennel? Christmas time is a time many families want to provide gifts of a special puppy or a kitten. However, fostering animals from a shelter can be a wonderful way to ensure your family is ready for such a commitment, while also providing opportunities for you to find the right pet match for your family. In addition, it can help you learn if someone in your family has a pet allergy that may complicate the ability to commit to a pet long-term. There are also millions of animals throughout the United States who are waiting to find adoptive homes.

Another way to help an animal, and a family as well, could be to offer to watch their pet for them as they travel for the holidays.

Shelters in your area may also welcome volunteer work to walk dogs or sit with pets to help them grow more comfortable with people, along with donations of pet food or toys.

If you live in an area with cold winters, putting out feeders for birds and squirrels is another way to help care for animals.

Children: What can you do that can help ensure a pet or animal has a great Christmas this year? Do you have a pet that you can give more playtime and attention?

Once you, as a family, decide how you can best help meet the needs of an animal, your reward will be in seeing how ecstatic an animal can become when someone shows them how much they care.

Reminder: Pray over your prayer list today.

December 20ᵗʰ

> *And there were shepherds living out in the fields nearby, keeping watch over their flocks at night. An angel of the Lord appeared to them, and the glory of the Lord shone around them, and they were terrified. But the angel said to them, "Do not be afraid. I bring you good news that will cause great joy for all the people. Today in the town of David a Savior has been born to you; he is the Messiah, the Lord. This will be a sign to you: You will find a baby wrapped in cloths and lying in a manger."*
>
> Luke 2:8-12

Although this passage mentions the birth of Jesus, for today's challenge, we are going to focus on the shepherds.

As we can see in this passage from Luke, an angel shared joyful, exciting news with the shepherds. If we read on in Luke 2:16-20, we can see that the shepherds, after seeing baby Jesus, also went about the land spreading the joyful, great news of Jesus's birth.

For today's challenge, what joyful, great news can you help share with others? Can you and your family go around your neighborhood singing Christmas Carols? Can you invite someone to a special event at your church? Can you tell someone about Jesus, who He is, and how much He loves them?

Children: Is there someone at your school you can invite to a fun activity at your church? Sometimes, when a child invites another child to church, the other child's parents begin to attend as well. Therefore, just by inviting one person, you may help positively influence the lives of several other family members as well. What better time is there to learn about Jesus than during the Christmas season?

Can you let them know how much you love and care about them as well? John 15:12 states, "*My command is this: Love each other as I have loved you.*"

What can you, individually or as a family, do today to let someone know how much you love them and how much they are loved by God? This could be one of the greatest gifts you can give someone. Please do this in a very loving, patient, non-judgmental way, as not everyone will be in a place in their lives where they are ready to receive this message.

Reminder: Pray over your prayer list today.

December 21ˢᵗ

> *Now after Jesus was born in Bethlehem of Judea in the days of Herod the king, behold, wise men from the East came to Jerusalem, saying, "Where is He who has been born King of the Jews? For we have seen His star in the East and have come to worship Him."*
>
> Matthew 2:1-2
>
> *When they saw the star, they rejoiced with exceedingly great joy. And when they had come into the house, they saw the young Child with Mary His mother, and fell down and worshiped Him. And when they had opened their treasures, they presented gifts to Him: gold, frankincense, and myrrh.*
>
> Matthew 2:10-11

For our challenge today, we will focus on the gifts that the wise men brought to Jesus.

The gift of "gold" is a symbolic way of demonstrating that the wise men recognized and accepted the status of Jesus as "King." Frankincense and myrrh were also gifts that were befitting of a king. They are anointing oils that can be used as incense for their fragrance or as perfume. Ironically, they can also be used for burials, which could be symbolic for what would happen later in Jesus's life.

However, did you also know that frankincense and myrrh are known for their medicinal purposes as well? Frankincense and myrrh, as essential oils, have been known to help alleviate pain from inflammation, arthritis, swelling, asthma, and to reduce the signs of aging.

With such medicinal purposes in mind, our challenge for today will focus on health and well-being.

As a family, can you brainstorm ideas for how to help someone you know who may be fighting an illness? Can you make them a hot meal, provide them company, or help them clean their house? Do they have staggering medical bills for which you may be able to help them raise money? Can you comfort someone by being a good listener? Can you imagine having to spend Christmas alone due to the misfortune of becoming ill?

Children: Is there someone you know who has been sick who would love to receive a get-well card from you?

Is there anything you and your family can do to strive to become the best, healthiest versions of yourselves this Christmas? If each of you can help support one another, such goals can be easier to achieve. Don't our loved ones deserve the best versions of ourselves we can give them?

Reminder: Pray over your prayer list today.

December 22nd

> *Do you not know that your bodies are temples of the Holy Spirit, who is in you, whom you have received from God? You are not your own; you were bought at a price. Therefore honor God with your bodies.*
>
> .
>
> 1 Corinthians 6:19-20

We are only a few days away from Christmas Day. Congratulations on making it this far on our kindness journey!

For today, we will pause, reflect, and give ourselves a little self-love and care. Just as we want to show kindness to others, it is also important to be kind to ourselves.

As we discussed in yesterday's challenge, our families deserve the best version of ourselves that we can give them.

When we read the passage above, it would be easy to infer that "bodies" is referring to our physical body and physical health. However, our mental and spiritual well-being is also a part of who we are. How can we be all that God would have us to be, or give our family our best selves, if we do not nurture our physical health, *as well as* our mental and spiritual health?

So, for today, while we take a moment to rest and refresh from our busy holiday season, what are some things you can do to nurture yourself today?

Can you go for a walk, do some yoga stretches, or listen to relaxing music? Can you soak in a warm bath, sit by a warm fire with your favorite book and, perhaps, a cup of hot chocolate? Can you get a manicure or get your hair done? Can you spend time playing your favorite game or sport?

Children: Can you go in your room and play quietly, or read a book, so your mom or dad can catch up on some rest they need to recharge their batteries before Christmas Day? This would also be the perfect time for you to make them a surprise picture, card, or note.

What can you do today to ensure that each person in your family does something today that is comforting and nurturing for them?

Reminder: Pray over your prayer list today.

December 23rd

Anyone who does not provide for their relatives, and especially for their own household, has denied the faith and is worse than an unbeliever.

1 Timothy 5:8

But the fruit of the Spirit is love, joy, peace, forbearance, kindness, goodness, faithfulness, gentleness and self-control. Against such things there is no law.

Galatians 5:22-23

Have you ever heard the expression, "charity begins at home?" 1 Timothy 5:8 is one verse where such an expression comes from, though, for the purpose of our discussion and book, we will interpret "charity" to mean "kindness."

Today's challenge will involve taking a closer look at how we are treating members of our family and household. None of us are perfect, as we all make mistakes, but, if we become upset, yell, scream, or throw things, are we practicing "gentleness and self-control" that are among the fruits of the spirit mentioned in Galatians 5:23?

If we discourage a loved one from following their dreams, which are hopefully based on the purpose God has placed them here to fulfill, are we practicing "faithfulness?"

Parents, the Bible teaches us, in Proverbs 22:6, to "*start children off in the way they should go and even when they are old, they will not turn from it.*" However, we cannot merely tell them lessons about God and the fruits of the spirit; we must also show them through our own actions and leadership.

Children, sometimes we can get upset and say hurtful things to our parents, sometimes without even meaning to or realizing it. But, if we are always striving to be kind, our words and actions should never hurt someone we love.

Our time on Earth is short, in comparison to the infinity of time. We are never promised a tomorrow here on Earth, so we never know how much time we will be blessed with to enjoy our loved ones. We may never be granted the opportunity to take back hurtful things we say or do. This could be why Ephesians 4:26 teaches us to never let the sun go down on our anger, which means, to never go to bed mad at someone. We can even take this a step further to say: Never leave the house angry.

For today's challenge, please take this opportunity to let your loved ones know how much they mean to you. Tell each other what you love most about one another. If you have trouble saying this aloud, consider writing a letter that conveys how much you care.

Children: Can you draw a special picture that shows your loved ones how much they mean to you, or write them a special note or letter?

If you use your creativity, there are a multitude of other ways to let your loved ones know how much they mean to you. Letting someone know how much you cherish them is a wonderful Christmas gift that will not easily be forgotten.

Reminder: Pray over your prayer list today.

December 24th

> **Give thanks to the Lord, for he is good; his love endures forever.**
>
> 1 Chronicles 16:34

We have made it to Christmas Eve, the day before we celebrate the birth of Jesus. Our kindness journey, for the purposes of this book, is nearly over. Thus far, we have shown kindness to strangers, neighbors, animals, ourselves, and our loved ones. Through it all, we have honored God with our actions and our attitudes regarding kindness and how to treat others the way we would like to be treated. However, what have we done to directly show kindness to God?

In the passage above, we can see that we need to spend time thanking God. We often pray for God to help meet a need for ourselves or someone else, but how often do we remember to take the time to thank God?

When I was a little girl, I recall my grandma singing a song that has always stuck with me. This song, "Thank You Lord for Your Blessings on Me," was originally written by James Easter and his brothers in 1954.

Here is the chorus of this simple, but powerful, moving song:

"There's a roof up above me
I've a good place to sleep
There's food on my table
And shoes on my feet
You gave me Your love, Lord
And a fine family
Thank You, Lord
For Your blessings on me"

As we go through the business of life, it can be easy to take our blessings for granted, and to not take the time to thank God for what we have.

Our challenge for today is to take time to thank God for all he has given us and has provided for us.

On this Christmas Eve, there may be churches in your area who are holding services that you could attend. Some do late night candlelight services as well on Christmas Eve. There may also be a choir performance today that you and your family could attend.

Children: Could you say a prayer thanking God for your food, your friends, your home, and your loved ones today?

After you spend some time today thanking God, please also take time today to enjoy your family God has blessed you with. If you are reading this book without a family surrounding you, sometimes God places special friends in our path to be our "family."

Whichever the case may be for you, on this Christmas Eve, may you find joy, peace, and happiness in all that you do.

Reminder: Pray over your prayer list today.

December 25th

> *So Joseph also went up from the town of Nazareth in Galilee to Judea, to Bethlehem the town of David, because he belonged to the house and line of David. He went there to register with Mary, who was pledged to be married to him and was expecting a child. While they were there, the time came for the baby to be born, and she gave birth to her firstborn, a son. She wrapped him in cloths and placed him in a manger, because there was no guest room available for them.*
>
> Luke 2:4-7

Merry Christmas! The day we have been waiting for is finally here. Today, we celebrate the birth of Jesus, the first gift of Christmas.

In John 3:16, we are told, "*For God so loved the world that he gave his one and only son (Jesus), that whoever believes in Him shall not perish but have eternal life.*"

Jesus is a gift that was freely given, by God himself, to each one of us, not because we deserved this gift, or because we did something to earn it, but as God's way of showing us just how much He loves us.

As we celebrate the birth of Jesus today, may we also enjoy our time with our family and friends while being mindful to let them know how much we love them - and how much they are loved by God.

May each gift we give and receive reflect our kindness, generosity, thankfulness, and, most importantly, serve as a reminder for how grateful we are for the precious gift of Jesus that God gave us and the world.

Happy Birthday, Jesus!

Merry Christmas, and God bless you! May His love, through your acts of kindness, show brightly through you in the year to come.

Author's Note

Thank you for taking this kindness journey with me, as we counted the days until Christmas. My sincere wish is that this book helped bring your family closer together, while also helping to put a smile on someone's face.

I hope this book helped you and your family put the "Christ" back in "Christmas," and I hope at least some of the prayers on your prayer list were answered as you progressed through this journey.

I also hope you found the prayer list page, and the following brainstorming pages helpful as well.

If you and your family enjoyed reading this book, and/or you would like to share stories or photos of some of the acts of kindness this book inspired you to do, please feel free to share them with me at: inspiredbyangel2@gmail.com. I would love to hear everything about them.

Sincerely,

Angel Williams
Author

Resource Section

In this section, you will find workspace for your prayer list, brainstorming, and more. You may wish to make copies of these pages, before use, if using this book in a group setting, or if you would like to use this book as an annual family tradition.

December 1st - Prayer List

Who to pray for:	Prayer Need:

December 2 - Supporting Single Mothers

December 3rd - Grief and Loss

December 4th - Supporting Fathers

December 5th - Supporting Married Couples

December 6th - Acts of Kindness and Patience

December 7th - Forgiveness

December 8th - The Golden Rule

December 9th - Cheerful Giver

December 10th - Transportation

December 11th - Food for the Hungry

December 12th - Drink for the Thirsty

December 13th - Clothing

December 14th - Shoes

December 15th - Providing Warmth

| |
| |
| |
| |
| |
| |
| |
| |

December 16th - Widows and Orphans

December 17th - Random Acts of Kindness

| |
| |
| |
| |
| |
| |
| |
| |

December 18th - Shelter and Hospitality

December 19th - Caring for Animals

December 20th - Sharing the Love of Christ

December 21st - Health and Wellness

December 22nd - Self Love and Care

December 23rd - Kindness to Family

December 24th - Thanking God

December 25th - Christmas Day Planning List

Special Event Reminder List

ABOUT THE AUTHOR

Angel Williams, a former teacher, is an aspiring author who resides in central Missouri. She and her husband, Dennis, were married just shy of 26 years before she became a widow. She is the proud mother of her 8-year-old son. She and her husband finalized his adoption from foster care just over a year before her husband passed away.

Aside from her desire to be the best possible mother she can be for her son, her dream is to spread as much kindness and positivity as possible, which she strives to do through her writing.

Angel has written poetry since childhood, some of which has won awards. She also writes blog articles for her nonprofit, All For Family, and she has previously self-published a Children's Book, "Why Can't I See My Friends?"

This book, "Kindness Countdown to Christmas," is her 2nd published book.